BOOK ANALYSIS

Written by Mélanie Ackerman
Translated by Ciaran Traynor

The Guernsey Literary and Potato Peel Pie Society

BY MARY ANN SHAFFER AND ANNIE BARROWS

Bright
≡Summaries.com

MARY ANN SHAFFER AND ANNIE BARROWS

A JOINT WORK

- **Mary Ann Shaffer was an American author who was born in Martinsburg, USA in 1934 and died in 2008. She is the author of:**
  - *The Guernsey Literary and Potato Peel Pie Society* (2008)
- **Annie Barrows is an American novelist who was born in San Diego, USA in 1962. Some of her notable works include:**
  - *The Magic Half* (2007), children's novel
  - *Ivy and Bean* (2008), children's novel
  - *The Guernsey Literary and Potato Peel Pie Society* (2008), novel

Mary Ann Shaffer was born in the USA in 1934. She was an editor, librarian and book shop employee. Her jobs in the book industry led her to write a novel based on the publishing world. After a trip to London, she set off for Guernsey and was immediately fascinated by the fact that the island was formerly under German occupation, to such an extent that she later decided to make it the setting of her story.

She spent several years writing the book. However, when her health began to decline she turned to her niece, Annie Barrows, a children's author, for help. She died in 2008 before managing to see her first and only book published and go on to become a bestseller.

THE GUERNSEY LITERARY AND POTATO PEEL PIE SOCIETY

AN ABSOLUTELY DELICIOUS NOVEL

- **Genre**: Epistolary novel
- **Reference Edition**: Barrows, A. and Shaffer, M. A. (2008) *The Guernsey Literary and Potato Peel Pie Society*. London: Bloomsbury.
- **1st edition**: 2008
- **Themes**: literature, reading, WWII, writing, love

The Guernsey Literary and Potato Peel Pie Society is an epistolary novel: in other words, a book made up of an exchange of letters. The novel was published in (American) English after the death of Mary Ann Shaffer in 2008.

Through a series of letters, the novel tells the story of a London-based woman writer's encounter with the inhabitants of the island of Guernsey. The Second World War has just come to an end, and everyone is still suffering from the effects of this difficult time. Through the letters that are exchanged, the reader not only learns what happened in the Channel Islands, but also finds out more about the life of lovers of reading.

SUMMARY

THE LITERARY SOCIETY

Juliet Ashton, a young English writer, is travelling around England to promote her book. Although she loves her job, she is painfully aware of its drawbacks, especially since she would like meet up with her friend Sophie, the sister of her editor Sidney Stark.

One day, after receiving flowers from a certain Markham Reynolds, she asks her editor to find out who he is. She learns that he is a rich American heir who works in newspaper publishing. Juliet then gets in contact with him and he ends up inviting her to dinner. The young woman falls under his spell from the moment she sets eyes on him, and they subsequently begin to go out in public together. Some time later, Markham asks her to marry him, but Juliet turns him down.

Meanwhile, a man called Dawsey Adams writes to Juliet to ask her some questions about the English writer Charles Lamb (1775-1834). He is in fact the new owner of one of Lamb's books, *Selected Essays of Elia,* which once belonged to Juliet and on which her name and address had been noted. He and Juliet then begin a correspondence about the Guernsey Literary and Potato Peel Pie Society, of which he is a member. Dawsey asks his friends Amelia Maugrey, Isola Pribby, Eben Ramsey, and John Bookeret to write to Juliet as well, and they all describe their relationship with reading to her. In this way, Juliet learns much about the inhabitants of the island and what they are reading during the Occupation. From these letters, Juliet discovers that the war forced families to split up and that some of the island's children were sent off to England before the arrival of the Germans, while certain inhabitants used their wits to survive. She also learns that Elizabeth, the founder of the society, was arrested and sent to the Ravensbrück concentration camp. Deeply moved by these stories, she decides to dedicate an article to them for *The Times*.

Juliet also receives letters from a woman called Adelaïde, a bitter old spinster who intends to sabotage Juliet's article by condemning the literary society. She takes her criticism one step further in targeting Elizabeth, whose daughter Kit is the fruit of an affair with Christian Hellman, a German. But Dawsey, who introduced the couple to one another, reveals that the couple were truly in love with one another. The society is quick to respond. After trying to Damage the reputation the members of the Society, Adelaïde is then targeted herself by Isola, a member of the society who is as eccentric as she is lovable. In spite of this background squabbling, Juliet writes her article, and her correspondents are very happy with it.

A BOOK ABOUT ELIZABETH

Juliet announces to her correspondents that she wishes to leave for Guernsey in order to meet the members of the Society. The news is met with enthusiasm from all, except from Markham, who tries to convince her to stay in England. However, Juliet, driven by her desire to meet up with her new friends, stands her ground for the first time. While waiting for her to arrive, the island's inhabitants prepare Elizabeth's cottage for the writer.

On arriving in Guernsey, Juliet discovers the faces that she had imagined through the letters, particularly Dawsey's, her first contact in Guernsey, who she describes very tenderly and at great length. With the exception of Kit, Elizabeth's daughter, everyone is delighted by her arrival. However, Juliet manages to win over even her with a joke on the very first day. Kit is surprised and becomes very fond of the young woman.

Once she arrives at Elizabeth's home, Juliet cannot help but begin to admire the other woman, who is praised at great length by the other inhabitants of the island and has been missing since her arrest. Juliet also attends a meeting of the Guernsey Literary and Potato Peel Pie Society, during which the main speaker verbally attacks another member of the group. At the same time, she begins work on her new novel.

Meanwhile, the island hears word from Remy, a former prisoner of the Ravensbrück camp, that Elizabeth has passed away, which comes as a great shock to the whole of Guernsey. Dawsey and Amelia decide to meet Remy in Normandy. While they are gone, the task of looking after Kit falls to Juliet. The writer, who is struggling to make progress with her new book, asks Sidney for advice. The editor therefore comes to visit Guernsey to help her out. In the meantime, Juliet's friend Isola, a member of the Society with an inquisitive nature, questions the editor on his relationship with Juliet. During the discussion, Sidney denies being in love with Juliet, since he is actually gay.

After reading the first few chapters of Juliet's book, Sidney makes her see the real subject of her work: instead of exploring the Occupation, she is actually concentrating on the character at the centre of the Literary Society – Elizabeth. From that point onwards, Juliet begins to focus more on this unknown woman, gathering accounts from those who knew her. As for Dawsey, he manages to convince Remy to come to Guernsey. As he is leaving to meet her, he and Juliet share an intimate moment which is interrupted by the arrival of Markham. Markham's intrusion leads the young woman to come to terms with her feelings, and she puts an end to their relationship the very next day. Remy arrives on the island and life goes back to normal: Juliet continues to look after Kit in the cottage and still regularly sees Amelia, Isola and even Dawsey, although he is no longer quite so friendly with her since the sudden appearance of Markham, who clearly prevented the two from growing closer.

The methods of Miss Marple

As she prepares to speak during a Literary Society meeting, Isola loses the notes she took during her reading and improvises, telling a story about her grandmother. She quickly phones Juliet, who discovers that some of the letters which Granny Pheen received and which were kept by Isola are signed O. F. O'F. W. W, possibly the signature of Oscar Wilde (Irish writer, 1854-1900). This is then confirmed by an expert. Sidney sends his secretary, whom Kit is immediately suspicious of, to fetch the letters. Susan Scott, one of Sidney's colleagues, intervenes to prove that the child is right: the secretary is actually working for a journalist who wants to tarnish the young woman's reputation. Thankfully, she is stopped in time.

Juliet makes two decisions which will turn her life upside down: adopting Kit and moving to Guernsey. She does, however, seem dismayed to find Remy with Dawsey, which Sidney takes as a sign that she is in love with Dawsey. Isola, who has a great admiration for Miss Marple, the heroine of Agatha Christie's novels (British writer, 1890-1976), decides to use her methods of behavioural observation to make Juliet understand her feelings for Dawsey. If Juliet was truly convinced that Dawsey and Remy were in love, this is mostly because she chose to think so rather than deducing it from evidence and objective facts.

A party is planned for Sidney's return to Guernsey and Eben, one of the Literary Society's more discreet members, states that some happy news will be announced. Juliet is convinced that this is the chance Remy and Dawson have been waiting for in order to make their love official. However, the news ends up being nothing more than the fact that Remy is leaving for France. Nevertheless, Juliet continues to believe that they are in love, but that Dawsey is just too timid to admit his feelings to Remy. Isola later shares her findings with Juliet, who realises that she was wrong from the beginning: the objects that Dawsey holds dear are all memories of times he spent with Juliet, not with Remy. She then runs after Dawsey and asks him to marry her. He accepts, and Juliet informs Sidney that he has to come back to Guernsey to attend their wedding.

CHARACTER STUDY

Juliet Ashton

Juliet Ashton is the main character of the novel. She is in her thirties and is the author of the book *Izzy Bickerstaff Goes to War*. One day, she receives a letter from Dawsey, a resident of Guernsey, whose radically different experience of the Second World War intrigues her so much that she begins to correspond regularly with him. She is then sent letters from friends of Dawsey who, like him, are also residents of Guernsey and also belong to the Guernsey Literary and Potato Peel Pie Society. As they continue to exchange letters, a friendship begins to bud between her and her correspondents, motivating her to go visit them in order to write about their experiences under the Occupation.

Being a strong-willed woman, she does not think twice before leaving her partner Markham Reynolds for Guernsey, despite his protests to the contrary. Playful and loyal, especially towards her friend and editor Sidney, she takes perfectly to island life, even if she does have to go through a few personal upheavals on the way. One of these is her attachment to Kit, the daughter of the late Elizabeth who becomes her principal source of inspiration, and the other is Dawsey. As the story progresses, we see Juliet fall helplessly in love with the island of Guernsey and its inhabitants. Thanks to them, she begins to come out of her shell and become a gentler person while still keeping her ironic, mocking humour.

Sidney Stark

Sidney Stark is Juliet's editor as well as her friend. As a result, he very quickly warns her off her partner Markham Reynolds, for whom he harbours a certain dislike: as an editor, he is a little jealous and frightened to see his favourite author leave for America, while as a friend he distrusts the very charming Markham.

Professionally, he strikes exactly the right balance between protective friend (reinforced by the ten year age gap between them) and editor, which allows him to maintain a critical approach to the young woman's work. He also does not hesitate to criticise her when necessary: "Strings of anecdotes don't make a book. Juliet, your book needs a centre" (p. 174).

However, their relationship is purely professional and friendly. In fact, by revealing his homosexuality to Isola (which Juliet already knows about), he confirms that their relationship will remain platonic. Thanks to Juliet, he too succumbs to the charms of Guernsey and its residents (particularly Isola, who he stays with during his first visit) and takes a keen interest in little Kit, who he takes great pleasure in spoiling with presents from London.

Sophie Stark

Sophie Stark, Sidney's sister, is the childhood friend of Juliet. Even though she lives in Scotland, she remains her closest friend. She is the one in whom Juliet most often confides her setbacks in love: "I want so much to talk to you. I want you to tell me whether I should marry Mark Reynolds" (p. 116). The two friends are very fond of one another.

Even if we do not know what Sophie looks like today, the portrait Juliet paints of her friend at 13 highlights the affection she has for her: "[She was] Perfect, she had golden curls, big blue eyes and a sweet, sweet smile" (p. 105). The fact that Juliet is the godmother of Sophie's son Dominic further reinforces their mutual affection.

Markham Reynolds, Junior

A rich American editor, Markham Reynolds manages to seduce Sophie after courting her tirelessly. He is indeed a good-looking man, described as having a "tanned" complexion with "blue eyes" (p. 37), "tall and handsome, with a crooked smile and a chiselled jaw" (p. 117).

However, Sidney is not pleased with the relationship between Markham and his friend. Indeed, the charming socialite's real goal is to find himself a 'trophy wife', a role which he would be quite happy to give to Juliet. In a letter addressed to his sister, Sidney explains that "If she marries him, she'll spend the rest of her life on display at theatres and restaurants and she'll never write another book" (p. 169). Juliet, to a certain extent, predicts the exact same fate and even jokes about it ironically: "Are you absolutely certain you wouldn't rather be married to someone more tractable?" (p. 115). This sudden proposal shows to what extent her relationship, as well as Markham himself, are superficial. Despite a few questions and doubts which she tells to Sophie and Sydney, Juliet quickly grows to prefer the Channel Islands to him, and Dawsey even more so, especially since he is the exact opposite of Markham.

OVER AT THE GUERNSEY LITERARY SOCIETY

Elizabeth McKenna

The unspoken leader of the society, Elizabeth is the cool-headed one who has the idea of explaining why her friends are out after curfew with the existence of a harmless reading group. Indeed, on their way home after having dinner at Amelia Maugery's house, which lasted long into the night, the guests could all easily have been arrested by the Germans for being out after curfew and ignoring rationing orders. However, that was not counting on Elizabeth's intervention, with the shrewd use of an innocent literary gathering as an excuse when caught by the Germans. The next day, everything was put into place by Elizabeth to make the lie a reality.

Energetic, generous, loyal and sunny, Juliet discovers a new aspect to Elizabeth's personality with each letter she receives from the Guernsey residents. Indeed, she is a source of inspiration for all the members of the literary society. And although Elizabeth seems proud to Isola, she was also encouraging and funny to a teenager suffering from scabies: "Her being funny helped me in my darkest hour" (p. 125), she says. Remy, who met her in the concentration camp, makes a similar remark, praising the talent she had "for making us forget where we were for a small while" (p. 155).

Even ignoring the Society members' accounts, Juliet immediately feels a connection to Elizabeth as soon as she arrives in Guernsey, as well as to her house and – above all – her daughter, who she ends up adopting after the death of the girl's mother. Elizabeth's omnipresence on the island leads Juliet to pay homage to her by basing her book on the other woman's life

Christian Hellman

Christian Hellman, a former German officer, became Dawsey's friend (in particular thanks to their mutual admiration for Charles Lamb) and Elizabeth's lover, with whom he had a daughter, Kit. In Dawsey's words "he looked like the German you imagine - tall, blond hair, blue eyes except he could feel pain" (p. 146). Through this character, Shaffer and Barrows reject the black-and-white thinking that was all too common at the end of the war.

Kit

The daughter of Elizabeth and Christian Hellman, Kit is a lively, curious child who tends to be on guard with strangers. Since the disappearance of her mother, Elizabeth's friends have brought her up together. Although she is at first wary of Juliet, she quickly becomes very attached to her. From this point on the two characters share a certain understanding, to such an extent that Juliet ends up adopting the little grey-eyed child with "chubby little legs" and "dark curls" (p. 140), and "a look she gets when she is concentrating hard", (p. 112) that makes her look like Elizabeth.

Dawsey Adams

Dawsey Adams is the first resident of Guernsey to contact Juliet. Having just acquired a book which used to belong to the young woman, he contacts her to try and find a copy of another book. His letter piques Juliet's curiosity and she begins to correspond regularly with him, and over time they form a friendship. It is through him that Juliet makes the acquaintance of the other members of the society.

When she arrives at Guernsey, Juliet's lengthy description of Dawsey makes it very clear to Sidney, as well as to the reader, that the writer and the shy but considerate worker will eventually fall in love: she describes him as a man with "a steady gaze" and "the sweetest smile I have ever seen" (p. 140). Their romance has a happy ending, in spite of Juliet's fear that he prefers Remy to her. Realising that Dawsey is truly in love with her, thanks to nosy Isola's discoveries, Juliet rushes to find him and ask him to marry her, and he eagerly accepts.

Amelia Maugery

It is thanks to a dinner at Amelia's house that the society is involuntarily created, made up as an excuse to explain why her friends were out after curfew. An ageing woman with a strong sense of integrity, she is described by Juliet as "Small, thin-faced, [with a] lovely smile, [and] grey hair in plaits wound round her head" (p. 141). She is one of the first people to write to Juliet. She is also the one who, along with Dawsey, has the courage to face up to the survivor Remy's stories of Nazi brutality and the death of Elizabeth, among other things. Just like the other main members of the Society, she often looks after Kit after her mother's death.

Isola Pribby

The gatekeeper of the society, Isola describes herself as "tall and built of big bones" and as someone who "do[es] not have a pleasing appearance" (p. 48). But her exuberant (she lives with a goat and a female parrot) and sociable nature (she signs her very first letter to Juliet with "your friend, Isola Pribby", p. 48; and throws herself into her arms when she first meets her with "Ah, lovey!", p. 140) make her someone as peculiar as she is lovable. Furthermore, she is the one to whom Juliet first admits, rather casually, her affection for the Guernsey residents: "And then – I began writing letters to strangers in Guernsey, now friends, whom I would indeed like to come and see" (p. 106).

When she is not taking care of Kit, she can be found trying to cook up strange potions, unlock the mysteries of 'the science of head bumps' and observe people's behaviour after the fashion of Miss Marple.

Remy Giraud

Remy is Elizabeth's final friend, who she met in Ravensbrück concentration camp. Although she appears quite late, Remy plays an important part in the story: it is through her that the Society learns what happened to Elizabeth. Her story serves as the main account of Nazi brutality. In describing her, Amelia comments that "her eyes are enormous and haunted. You can see that she was a beauty in better times, but now – she is like glass" (p. 163). The use of the expression "in better times" implies that her beauty vanished long ago, which is all the more tragic since Remy is only 24 years old.

Since she has no ties or obligations, she heads to Guernsey in honour of her friendship with Elizabeth, where she is welcomed with open arms, particularly by Dawsey, which of course makes Juliet jealous.

John Booker

John Booker is one of the founding members of the Society. Being a little the worse for wear, he could not keep quiet on the way home from Amelia's dinner, alerting the Germans that the guests were out after curfew. A former servant who stole the identity of a lord on the run from the Germans, John Booker is first introduced as a comical character whose main concern in life is alcohol. Although he is Jewish, we find out that Elizabeth advised him against reporting this to the German authorities. It is only shortly before the second part of the book that another side to his character is revealed. After being given up to the authorities, he is sent first to the Neuengamme and then to the Belsen concentration camps. However, he was deported not for being a Jew, but for pretending to be a noble. The Germans did not take kindly to being fooled. His account is the one which first introduces Nazi brutality into the story, well before Remy gives her version of events, and it is this which forces Juliet to confront the reality of the concentration camps: "What we were – it wasn't dead, but it wasn't alive either [...] so after we'd dug long trenches, we pulled and dragged the bodies to the edges and threw them in" (pp. 130-131).

ANALYSIS

THE THEME OF WAR

In 1946, Juliet comes into contact with a group of islanders. Through the letters that she exchanges with them, the reader is introduced to the events of the Second World War through the eyes of those who lived through them. Some of the topics which are touched upon are:

- **Fear**. The residents have to endure blockades, food shortages, living together with the Germans, curfew, etc.
- **Absence of children**. Having already left for England before the arrival of the Germans, they do not come back until 5 years later.
- **Being arrested and sent to concentration camps.** This is the fate reserved for Elizabeth, who was deported to Ravensbrück for helping a slave. The Nazi regime had indeed resorted to slavery, as Amelia explains in a letter to Juliet: "I have recently learnt that their inhuman treatment was the deliberate policy of Himmler. He called his plan Death by Exhaustion, and he implemented it" (p. 93).
- **The relationships which formed with the occupiers.** Elizabeth, for example, began to see Christian, a German soldier, with whom she eventually had a child.

All of this information is completely new to Juliet, whose only experience of the war was the Blitz.

Through the stories told by the residents, the reader uncovers a deeply human message behind the book: the enemy is not always who you think they are. The islanders of Guernsey learned this the hard way, as certain people that they had known their whole life were prepared to do anything to look good in the eyes of the German authorities, even going so far as to give up their neighbours. On the other hand, certain Germans turned out to be kind to the island's residents. In doing this, Shaffer and Barrows are trying to look at war in a different light and debunk the black-and-white view of the war with the good French people on one side, victims of the war, and the totally evil Germans on the other.

THE WORLD OF BOOKS

The novel is peppered with numerous allusions to literature, which take on different forms.

The Literary Society

As the title of the book implies, the story is focused on a literary society. Generally speaking, a literary society refers to a group of literature enthusiasts who meet up to talk about and discuss reading and other similar subjects. This tradition goes back centuries. In Shaffer and Barrow's story, the society in question is on the island of Guernsey. It was set up during the Second World War and continues after the end of the conflict. The idea to found this sort of group came from the circumstances at the time, since it was thought up by Elizabeth and some of Amelia's guests to avoid trouble with the Germans.

LITERARY SOCIETIES

Literary societies or literary salons appeared in France in the 17th century. Often run by women, they were a place for the intellectual elite to meet and share ideas. Eloquence was extremely important, and Marie de Rabutin-Chantal, better known as Madame de Sévigné (French writer, 1626-1696) was a perfect example of this. During the Age of Enlightenment in the 18th century, the main topics of discussion were not only literature, but also philosophy and science, domains which advocated the intellectual advancement of man over the obscurantism which had been the norm in the previous centuries. Finally, in the 19th century, a female figure, Juliette Récamier (1777-1849) would once again find herself at the centre of the most illustrious people of society (or those who would soon be among them), including Chateaubriand (1768-1848), Lamartine (1790-1869) and Balzac (1799-1850).

In this way, the members of the Society meet regularly to discuss their literary experiences and become friends. Reading allows the residents to forget life under the Occupation and, most importantly, stops them from becoming lonely. In a way, the Guernsey Literary and Potato Peel Pie Society allows some of the Guernsey residents to create a little society in the midst of the larger society at war.

The name of the society itself comes from the meal which led to the creation of the group: one of the members, a rather mad cook, had no intention of coming to the meeting if there were not going to be any refreshments. He therefore took it upon himself to bake a potato peel pie, which ended up being quite the success.

Juliet and the job of a writer

The main character's job as a writer is obviously a clear reference to the world of books. Shaffer and Barrows highlight two essential aspects of this profession:

- **The purely literary side**. The reader watches as Juliet searches for a subject for her new book. There is the usual myth of the writer who cuts themselves off from the outside world to write: Juliet decides to leave London for the Channel Islands in order to better understand how to write a novel about the Occupation. She is also motivated by other factors: her concern for objectivity, her need to put some distance between Markham and herself, and her affection for the members of the Society.
- **The extra parts of the job**. Writers do not write all the time: they also have to promote their books, do interviews which can sometimes be unpleasant, etc.

Publishers and bookshops

Stephens & Stark is the company which publishes Juliet's books, with Sidney as her editor. The way in which Sidney and Juliet's relationship is described highlights the depth of their friendship and their unwavering faith in each other. Juliet is also quite close with Susan Scott from the publishing house, who organises her book promotion tour. All this gives the impression that the editors are professionals who put their books and their authors first.

However, these characters are joined by publishing giants like Markham Reynolds, men who are more in love with money than books, which is something Sidney cannot abide. The novel also portrays Markham as a man whose only reason to get in to publishing was to "beguile England's finest authors" (p. 36). That being said, he does not try to convince Juliet to change publisher while he is going out with her. However, that is not to say that their relationship is particularly good for Juliet. In fact, when Mark comes to see her in Guernsey, he acts very selfishly, and Juliet thinks it best to break off the relationship.

Literary references

Besides the description of many literature-related activities, Shaffer and Barrows include many different literary references in their novel. These include:

- **The British writer Charles Lamb (1775-1834)**. He is the most significant reference in the novel. It is thanks to him that Juliet established links with Dawsey and Guernsey. He also continues to crop up throughout the story.
- **The Brontë sisters (Charlotte, 1816-1855; Emily, 1818-1848; Anne, 1820-1849)** are also repeatedly mentioned throughout the book, which is rather noteworthy. They symbolise the passionate love which Isola so admires, as well as of a certain kind of feminine pride.
- **Many other writers.** Although they occupy a more secondary role in the text, a number of them are still

present. Among the authors mentioned are Jane Austen, (1775-1817), William Wordsworth (1770-1805), Charles Dickens (1812-1870) and Agatha Christie.

Reading as a popular pastime

When it first came out, *The Guernsey Literary and Potato Peel Pie Society* was considered a mainstream success. The use of the adjective "mainstream" is interesting. The style and vocabulary that are used are certainly informal, but it is above all in the portraits made of the Society's members that we realise that the book is a love letter to both reading and to ordinary people. None of the Society's members are of high social standing. The servant John Booker is fascinated by the letters of Seneca (4 BC-AD 65), the fisherman Eben Ramsey greatly admires Shakespeare (1564-1616), while the farmer Clovis Fossey woos his future wife thanks to the poet Wilfred Owen (1893-1918). While at first the contrast between ancient or classic authors and ordinary people seems rather amusing, the reader soon realises that reading actually symbolises the resistance of Guernsey's inhabitants. In this way, the islanders highlight the critical importance of culture and reading in the face of the barbaric, book-burning Nazis. On the other hand, the novel depicts the upper classes in a very critical manner. Markham Reynolds, the extremely rich American publisher, is portrayed as a proud socialite, while the journalist Gilly Gilbert and her partner Billy Bee are driven only by deceit and their desire for revenge.

With *The Guernsey Literary and Potato Peel Pie Society*, Mary Ann Schaffer and Annie Barrows try to change the idea that reading is only for the enjoyment of the elite and offer a touching portrayal of ordinary people.

An epistolary novel

Epistolary writing involves a correspondence or an exchange in written form. The practice goes back to antiquity, when authors such as Seneca were already writing letters. However, the concept of an epistolary genre did not appear until the 16th century as it was only at this time that printing had advanced enough to allow exchanged letters to be published.

There are several types of writings which can be classified as epistolary works: "Authentic letters published later on become literature without intending to [...], while on the other hand there are works of fiction which are made out to be private correspondences which just happened to be found in an attic somewhere[...]"[1] (*Le Dictionnaire du littéraire*, pp. 195-197). In this second category we can find two noteworthy works:

- The *Lettres provinciales* by Blaise Pascal (French philosopher, 1623-1662). The writer chose the form of a letter in order to better construct his defence of Jansenism and of his friend Antoine Arnauld (French theologian, 1612-1694). He opted to use a pseudonym and published a collection of fictional missives.
- *Letters of a Portuguese Nun* (1969). These anonymously published letters were extremely successful. Long

---

1. This quotation has been translated by BrightSummaries.com.

considered to be the work of a nun talking to her lover, research finally revealed the author to be the viscount of Guilleragues (French diplomat and writer, 1628-1685).

Since then, epistolary novels have continued to be written and read with enthusiasm. One of the particularities of this type of writing is the use of "I" and the insight into the private lives of the letter-writers, who can be real of fictional.

The Guernsey Literary and Potato Peel Pie Society belongs to the second type of epistolary novel, seeing as it is made up of a series of fictional letters written by Shaffer and Barrows to create the impression of real correspondence. This is a very deliberate choice, as it allows the characters to talk about themselves and to confide in each other. Through these exchanges, it is possible to see the repetition of certain episodes, like the invention of the Literary Society. Since there are several characters involved in the exchanging of letters, the same events are told from different perspectives. This may, however, make the reader feel that the story is a little slow because correspondence implies a certain time gap between events, as things have to happen before they can be reported. We therefore never have a first-hand look at events.

When it was published in 2008, *The Guernsey Literary and Potato Peel Pie Society* met with considerable success. Its likeable characters and typical British humour allowed the book to remain on the prestigious *New York Times* Best Seller List for paperback trade fiction for 11 weeks.

FURTHER REFLEXION

SOME QUESTIONS TO THINK ABOUT...

- To what extent can we say *The Guernsey Literary and Potato Peel Pie Society* has an autobiographical component?
- In your opinion, what is the role of the many literary references in this story?
- In a postwar context, why would an author choose to write a story about the Occupation in an epistolary style?
- In one of her letters, Juliet says: "Perhaps there is some secret sort of homing instinct in books that brings them to their perfect readers" (p. 9). Do you think that this book is aimed at a certain type of reader in particular? How would you explain that?
- In one of her letters to Sidney, Juliet describes Kit's reaction to her arrival in Guernsey: "she didn't take to me one bit" (p. 140). How can the child's attitude be interpreted?
- To what extent can the characters be considered stereotypes? Use the examples of Juliet, Sidney, Markham Amelia, Dawsey and Isola to support your answer.
- How would you explain the difference between the brief exchanges between Markham Reynolds and Juliet and the lengthy letters between the writer and the members of the Literary Society?
- In terms of the action, do you notice a sort of evolution between the first and second part of the novel?
- Try to give a definition of "English humour", based on your reading of the book and your personal experience.
- When the French edition of the book came out, one of the comments on the cover said "Absolutely delicious".

What effect(s) could this have, particularly in terms of sales?

We want to hear from you!
Leave a comment on your online library
and share your favourite books on social media!

FURTHER READING

REFERENCE EDITION

- Barrows A. and Shaffer M. A. (2008) *The Guernsey Literary and Potato Peel Pie Society*. London: Bloomsbury.

www.brightsummaries.com

Ebook EAN: 9782806280435

Paperback EAN: 9782806294333

Legal Deposit: D/2017/12603/104

This guide was produced with the support of the Service general des Lettres et du Livre of the Fédération Wallonie-Bruxelles.

This guide was written with the collaboration of Célia Ramain for the 'Character study' and 'Reading as a popular pastime' sections.

Cover: © Primento

Digital conception by Primento, the digital partner of publishers.